We hope you will enjoy the Recovery Coloring Book!
For more please visit us online at www.hopeincolor.com

I thank God to whom I owe everything good in my life.
Thank you, Arody Victoria, for the beautiful illustrations! Special thanks to my family and friends for your love, support and inspiration. Mom and Dad, Bruce, Molly, Keath and Clifton. I dedicate this book to those special people dealing with mental or physical illnesses and their families. And my wish is for peace and love to everyone this book touches.
- Tom

Thank you Tom and Clifton for the opportunity and for believing in my work! As always thank you God, my great assistants Neyda, Ariana and Giancarlo and to all my family.
- Arody

Follow us on: recoverycoloringbook @color4fun

Sources:
The Holy Bible, World English Bible; eBible.org, 2015. http://www.ebible.org/web/.

The Book of Common Prayer. New York: Seabury Press, 1979.

COPYRIGHT © 2015 by Recovery Coloring Books, LLC.
All rights reserved by Recovery Coloring Books, LLC.

No part of this publication may be reproduced in whole or in part, or stored in a retrieval system, or transmitted in any form or by any means, electronic, mechanical, photocopying, recording, or otherwise, without written permission of the publisher.

ISBN: 978-0-9962817-0-6
First Edition. Dec., 2015

VOLUME 1

The Recovery Coloring Book

With Messages of Faith, Hope, and Healing

By
Tom Castelloe

Illustrated by
Arody J. Victoria

The Recovery Coloring Book

Coloring as an Alternative Form of Meditation

If you're suffering from stress, anxiety, illness, or addiction, you've probably heard that meditation can be a great way to ease your troubles and aid your recovery. Indeed, meditation is an excellent way to reach a peaceful state of mind, finding relief from stress and worry. Meditation can help you to relax, and it can help you to process thoughts and feelings you've been struggling with, whether consciously or unconsciously. For some people, however, meditation is difficult to get into. The lack of structure can make it hard to find peace and silence. Instead, you may feel distracted or impatient. If you struggle with traditional meditation, coloring can help you to find that same balanced peace. In fact, The Recovery Coloring Book has been designed to help you find calm and healing.

Think about the last time you colored. You were probably a child, and the act of coloring was a simple and happy activity. As an adult, coloring can bring back that simple sense of joy and creativity. A number of studies so far have found that coloring helps to relieve stress and anxiety in a way that's remarkably similar to meditation. Why does coloring work as meditation? It's largely because coloring is in essence a simple, repetitive action. It requires just enough focus to bring you into the present, enabling you to get some space away from worries and anxieties that have been troubling you. At the same time, the repetition means that your subconscious is free to work in the background. This can help you to process difficult thoughts and feelings, leaving you feeling less weighed down when you're done coloring. It's a kind of active meditation.

You can use coloring as an exercise much in the same way you would use meditation. As you color in the beautiful designs of this book, try to be entirely present in the moment. Think about the way your body feels. Pay attention to the way the color and design look on the page. If you find your mind wandering, you can also use the book's messages of faith, hope, and healing to guide your meditation. Take a moment to reflect on the biblical quotes and think about what they mean to you. These simple steps can convey the same benefits as meditation. In addition, coloring has the extra benefit of bringing out your creative side. Artistic activity naturally brings with it a sense of joy and excitement. Even if you don't think of yourself as much of an artist, coloring is a simple way to relish your own creativity. I hope that coloring in this book will help you to let go of stress, find a sense of peace, and relish a simple joy.

But the fruit of the Spirit is love, joy, peace, patience, kindness, goodness, faith, gentleness, and self-control.
— Galatians 5:22

The Recovery
Coloring Book

He will wipe away every tear from their eyes.
Death will be no more; neither will there be
mourning, nor crying, nor pain, any more.
The first things have passed away.
– Revelation 21:4

The Recovery
Coloring Book

"For I know the thoughts that I think toward you," says the Lord, "thoughts of peace, and not of harm, to give you hope and a future."

– Jeremiah 29:11

The Recovery
Coloring Book

Blessed be the God and Father of our Lord Jesus Christ, the Father of mercies and God of all comfort; who comforts us in all our affliction, that we may be able to comfort those who are in any affliction, through the comfort with which we ourselves are comforted by God.

– 2 Corinthians 1:4

www.recoverycoloringbook.com

The Recovery
Coloring Book

*Oh taste and see that the Lord is good.
Blessed is the man who takes refuge in him.*
— Psalm 34:8

The Recovery
Coloring Book

*I will sing of the loving kindness
of the Lord forever.
With my mouth, I will make known your
faithfulness to all generations.*
– Psalm 89:1

The Recovery
Coloring Book

The Lord is my strength and my shield.
My heart has trusted in him, and I am
helped. Therefore my heart greatly rejoices.
With my song I will thank him.
– Psalm 28:7

www.recoverycoloringbook.com

The Recovery
Coloring Book

The Lord is good to all.
His tender mercies are over all his works.
– Psalm 145:9

www.recoverycoloringbook.com

The Recovery
Coloring Book

𝓑ehold, God is my salvation. I will trust, and will not be afraid; for Yah, The Lord, is my strength and song; and he has become my salvation.

– Isaiah 12:2

The Recovery
Coloring Book

Come to me, all you who labor and are heavily burdened, and I will give you rest. Take my yoke upon you, and learn from me, for I am gentle and humble in heart; and you will find rest for your souls. For my yoke is easy, and my burden is light.
– Matthew 11:28 – 30

The Recovery
Coloring Book

Cast your burden on the Lord, and he will sustain you. He will never allow the righteous to be moved.
- Psalm 55:22

The Recovery
Coloring Book

So now faith, hope, and love abide, these three; but the greatest of these is love.
— 1 Corinthians 13:13

The Recovery
Coloring Book

God is our refuge and strength, a very present help in trouble.
— Psalm 46:1

The Recovery
Coloring Book

Trust in the Lord with all your heart, and don't lean on your own understanding. In all your ways acknowledge him, and he will make your paths straight.
— Proverbs 3:5-6

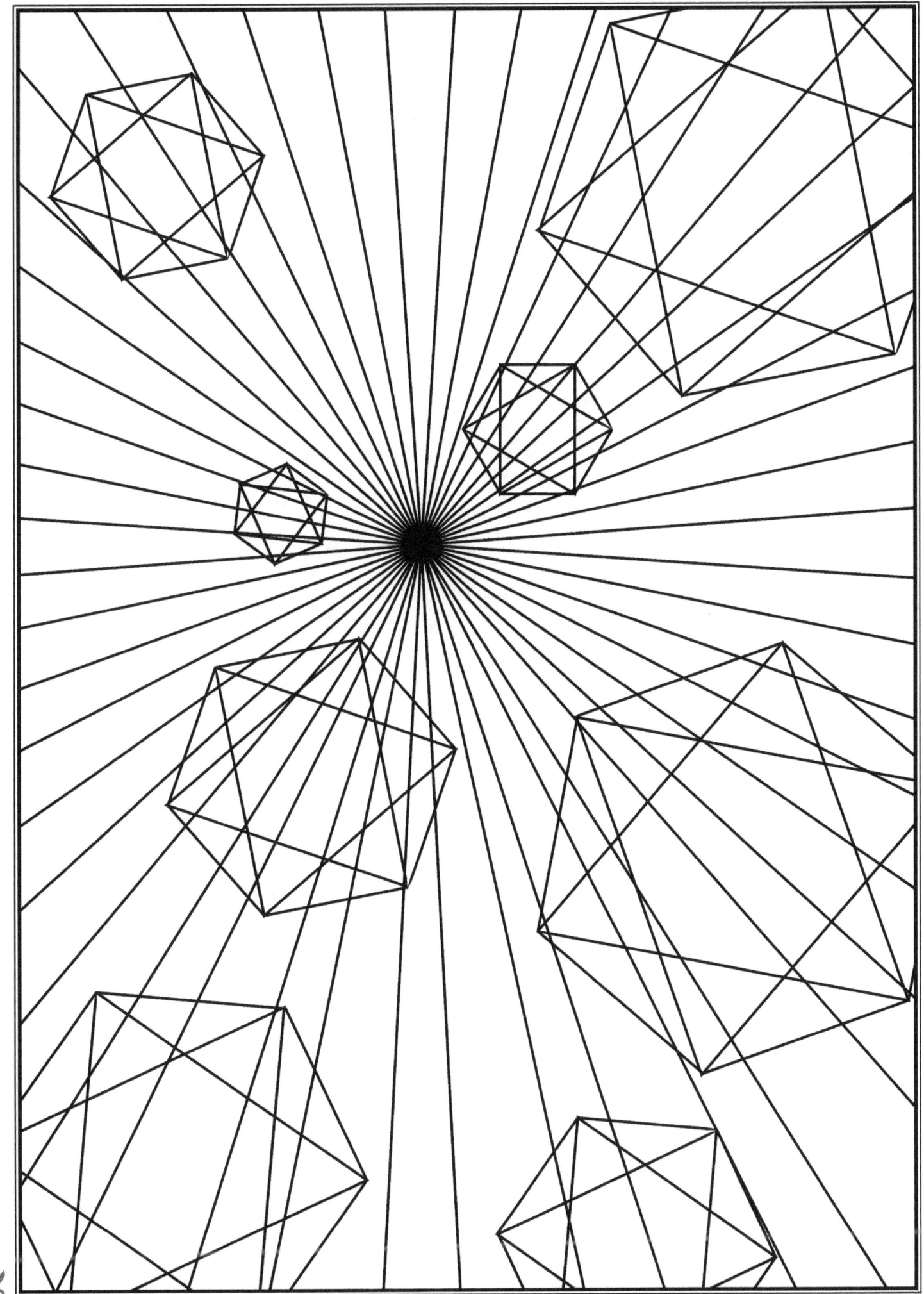

The Recovery
Coloring Book

For the Lord is good. His loving kindness endures forever, his faithfulness to all generations.
– Psalm 100:5

The Recovery
Coloring Book

Therefore if anyone is in Christ, he is a new creation. The old things have passed away. Behold, all things have become new.
– 2 Corinthians 5:17

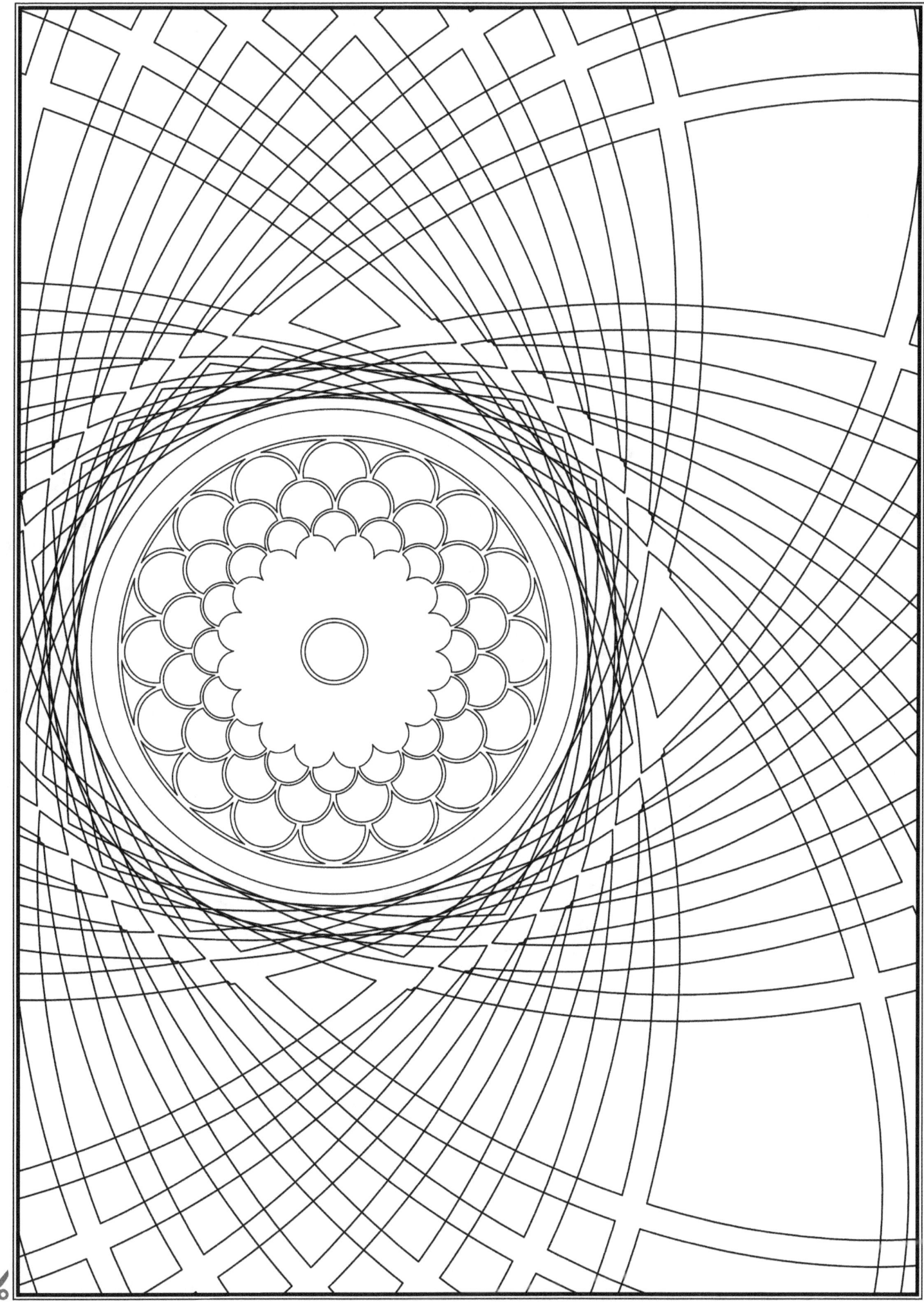

The Recovery
Coloring Book

The Lord is my shepherd: I shall lack nothing.
He makes me lie down in green
pastures. He leads me beside still waters.
He restores my soul.
He guides me in the paths of righteousness
for his name's sake.
Even though I walk through the valley of
the shadow of death, I will fear no evil, for
you are with me.
Your rod and your staff, they comfort me.
You prepare a table before me in the presence
of my enemies.
You anoint my head with oil.
My cup runs over.
Surely goodness and loving kindness shall
follow me all the days of my life, and I will
dwell in house of the Lord forever.
– Psalm 23:1-6

The Recovery
Coloring Book

Peace I leave with you. My peace I give to you; not as the world gives, give I to you. Don't let your heart be troubled, neither let it be fearful.
– John 14:27

The Recovery
Coloring Book

Behold, I am with you always, even
to the end of the age. Amen.
– Matthew 28:20

The Recovery
Coloring Book

*Your word is a lamp to my feet,
and a light for my path.*
– Psalm 119:105

www.recoverycoloringbook.com

The Recovery
Coloring Book

Be strong and courageous. Don't be afraid. Don't be dismayed, for Yahweh your God is with you wherever you go.
– Joshua 1:9

The Recovery
Coloring Book

*I can do all things through Christ,
who strengthens me.*
– Philippians 4:13

www.recoverycoloringbook.com

The Recovery
Coloring Book

Now faith is assurance of things hoped for, proof of things not seen.
– Hebrews 11:1

The Recovery Coloring Book

But those who wait for the Lord will
renew their strength.
They will mount up with wings like eagles.
They will run, and not be weary.
They will walk, and not faint.
– Isaiah 40:31

The Recovery
Coloring Book

Finally, brothers, whatever things are true, whatever things are honorable, whatever things are just, whatever things are pure, whatever things are lovely, whatever things are of good report; if there is any virtue, and if there is any praise, think about these things.
– Philippians 4:8

The Recovery
Coloring Book

In nothing be anxious, but in everything, by prayer and petition with thanksgiving, let your requests be made known to God. And the peace of God, which surpasses all understanding, will guard your hearts and your thoughts in Christ Jesus.

– Philippians 4:6-7

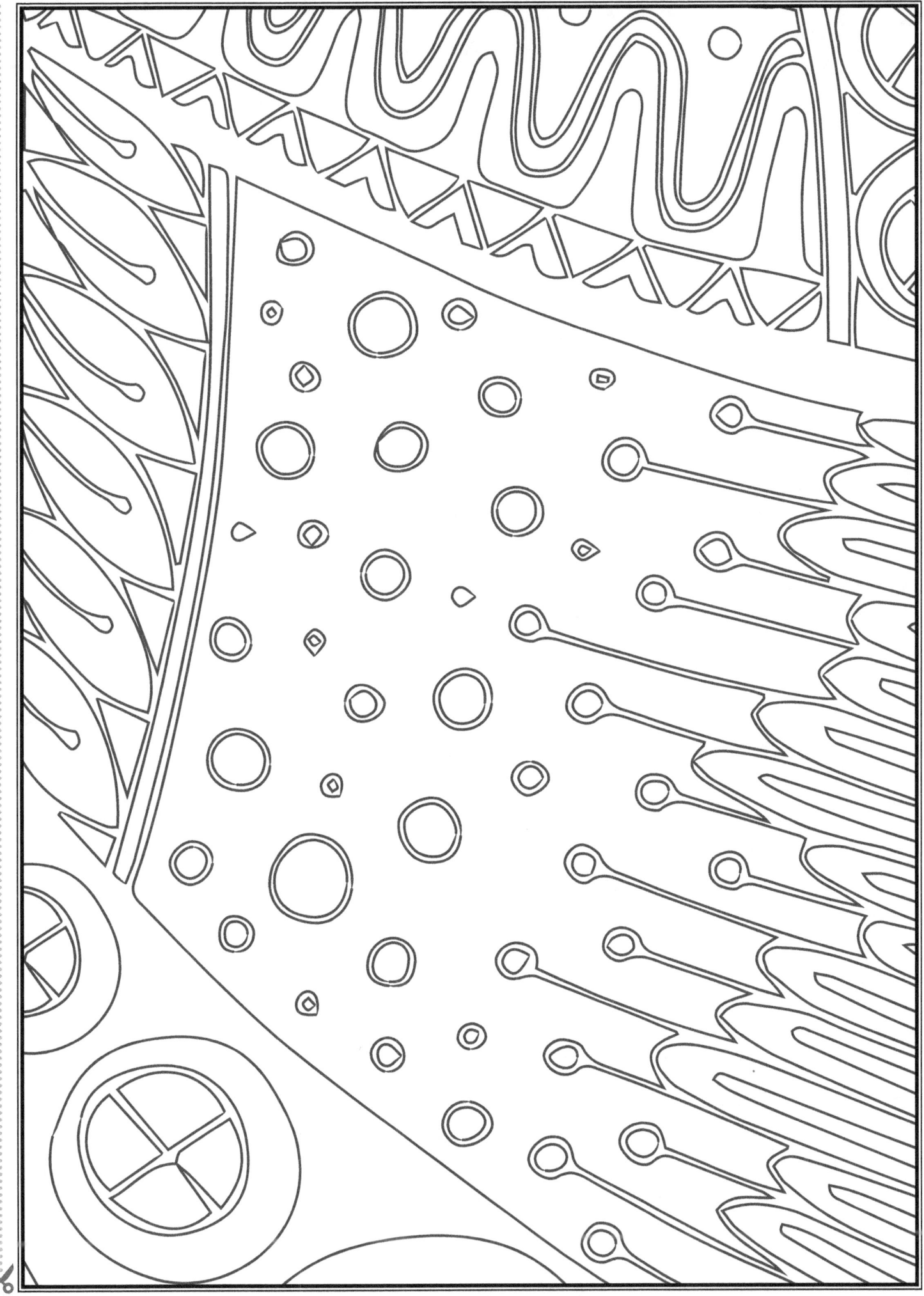

The Recovery
Coloring Book

Above all these things, walk in love, which is the bond of perfection.
　　　　　– Colossians 3:14

The Recovery
Coloring Book

This is the day that the Lord has made.
We will rejoice and be glad in it!
– Psalm 118:24

www.recoverycoloringbook.com

The Recovery
Coloring Book

He heals the broken in heart,
and binds up their wounds.
– Psalm 147:3

The Recovery
Coloring Book

Beloved, I pray that you may prosper in all things and be healthy, even as your soul prospers.
– 3 John 1:2

The Recovery
Coloring Book

The Lord is near to those who have
a broken heart, and saves those
who have a crushed spirit.
– Psalm 34:18

The Recovery
Coloring Book

Now may the God of hope fill you with all joy and peace in believing, that you may abound in hope, in the power of the Holy Spirit.

– Romans 15:13

The Recovery
Coloring Book

*Oh give thanks to the God of heaven;
for his loving kindness endures forever.*
– Psalm 136:26

The Recovery
Coloring Book

For I, the LORD your God, will hold your right hand, saying to you, 'Don't be afraid. I will help you.'
– Isaiah 41:13

The Recovery
Coloring Book

I trust in God's loving kindness forever and ever.
– Psalm 52:8b

The Recovery
Coloring Book

*For God didn't give us a spirit of fear,
but of power, love, and self-control.*
  – 2 Timothy 1:7

The Recovery
Coloring Book

For everything there is a season, and a time for every purpose under heaven.
  – Ecclesiastes 3:1

The Recovery
Coloring Book

Love is patient and is kind; love doesn't envy. Love doesn't brag, is not proud, doesn't behave itself inappropriately, doesn't seek its own way, is not provoked, takes no account of evil; doesn't rejoice in unrighteousness, but rejoices with the truth; bears all things, believes all things, hopes all things, endures all things.
– 1 Corinthians 13:4–7

The Recovery
Coloring Book

Lord's Prayer

Our Father, who art in heaven, hallowed be thy
Name, thy kingdom come, thy will be done, on
earth as it is in heaven.

Give us this day our daily bread.
And forgive us our trespasses, as we forgive those
who trespass against us.

And lead us not into temptation,
but deliver us from evil.

For thine is the kingdom, and the power, and the
glory, for ever and ever. Amen.

– Book of Common Prayer

The Recovery
Coloring Book

www.ingramcontent.com/pod-product-compliance
Lightning Source LLC
Chambersburg PA
CBHW080412300426
44113CB00015B/2488